HURON COUNTY LIBRARY
3 6492 00459388 2

D1214851

Animal Mummies:

Preserved through the Ages

by Charlotte Wilcox

Consultant:
Dr. Salima Ikram
Department of Egyptology
American University in Cairo

CAPSTONE
HIGH-INTEREST
BOOKS
an imprint of Capstone Press
Mankato, Minnesota

Capstone High-Interest Books are published by Capstone Press
151 Good Counsel Drive, P.O. Box 669, Mankato, Minnesota 56002
http://www.capstone-press.com

Printed in the United States of America.

Library of Congress Cataloging-in-Publication Data
Wilcox, Charlotte.
Animal mummies: preserved through the ages/by Charlotte Wilcox.
p. cm.—(Mummies)
Summary: Describes animal mummies, some of the most famous animal mummies and where they have been found, how animals are mummified, how scientists study them, and what they can teach us about the past.
Includes bibliographical references and index.
ISBN 0-7368-1305-5 (hardcover)
1. Mummified animals—Juvenile literature. 2. Animal remains (Archaeology)—Juvenile literature. [1. Mummies. 2. Animal remains (Archaeology)] I. Title. II. Series.
CC79.5.A5 W57 2003
393′ .3—dc21 2001007932

Editorial Credits
Carrie Braulick, editor; Karen Risch, product planning editor; Kia Adams, designer; Jo Miller, photo researcher

Photo Credits
AP/Wide World Photos, 24; Enric Marti, cover
Aurora, 12; Thomas Ernsting, 15
Barry McWayne/University of Alaska Museum, 10
Carl & Ann Purcell/CORBIS, 23
Nowitz/Folio, Inc., 16, 18
Reuters/Archive by Getty Images, 4, 6
Sandro Vannini/CORBIS, 21, 29
Sean Sexton Collection/CORBIS, 28
SOQUI TED/CORBIS SYGMA, 26

1 2 3 4 5 6 07 06 05 04 03 02

Table of Contents

Learn About:
- The Zharkov mammoth
- Locations of animal mummies
- Studying animal mummies

In 1997, two boys discovered tusks poking out of the frozen ground in Siberia.

Chapter One

A Mammoth Discovery

In spring 1997, two boys were herding reindeer in a part of northern Russia called Siberia. The boys were members of the Zharkov family.

A Mammoth Mummy

One of the boys saw a huge tusk poking out of the frozen ground. Nearby, the boys found another tusk. The tusks were attached to a large, hairy head. The boys thought it might be a mammoth's head. These animals looked like large, woolly elephants. Mammoths are extinct. They died out thousands of years ago.

The boys cut the tusks from the head. Two of the boys' family members brought the tusks to a market to sell. They met French explorer Bernard Buigues at the market. He asked the family members where they found the tusks. The family agreed to show Buigues the place.

In fall 1997, Buigues saw the woolly head. He knew the head belonged to a mammoth.

The Zharkov mammoth's tusks were very large.

Buigues made plans to dig the rest of the animal's remains out of the ice.

In fall 1999, Buigues and a team of workers arrived in Siberia. They chopped out a large block of ice around the mammoth.

The block of ice containing the mammoth weighed more than 20 tons (18 metric tons). A helicopter lifted the ice block to a cave in Khatanga. This city is located in northern Siberia.

Several scientists traveled to Khatanga to study the mummy. They learned the mammoth was 45 to 50 years old when it died. Scientists believe the mammoth died several thousand years ago. They named it the Zharkov mammoth.

Cloning

Scientists wanted to use DNA samples to clone the Zharkov mammoth. DNA is found in all living cells. It determines the physical features of animals and people.

Scientists planned to remove DNA from the mammoth's cells. They would place the DNA into an egg cell from an elephant. A mammoth exactly like the mummy would grow from the egg. But centuries in the ice destroyed too much DNA in the Zharkov mammoth's cells to try this procedure.

Animal Mummies

People have found animal mummies throughout the world. Conditions in both warm and cold climates can preserve dead bodies.

Animal mummies can help scientists learn about the past. Scientists may learn about how animals once lived or about how their features

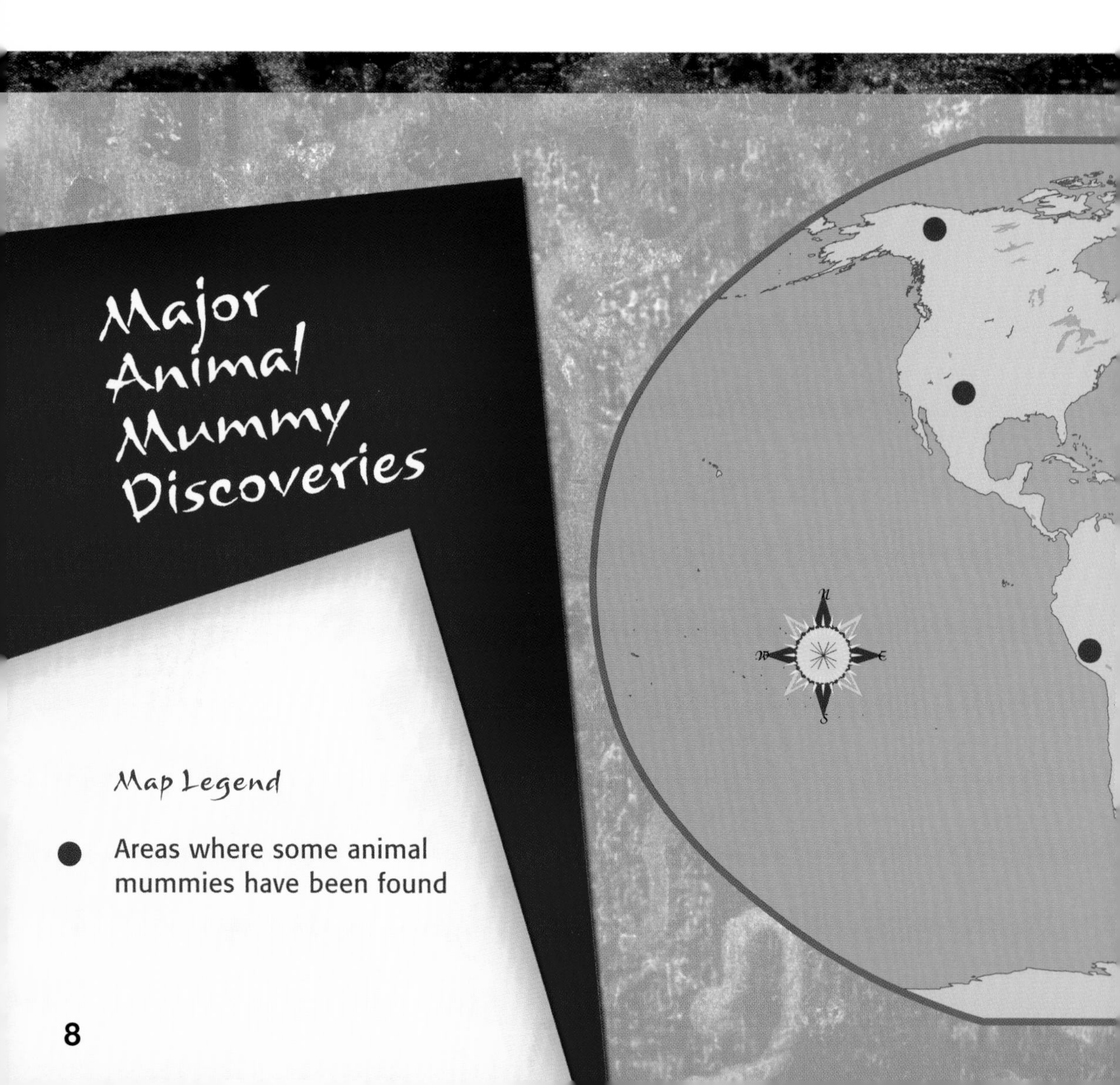

have changed over time. Animal mummies also can help scientists learn about ancient groups of people.

Scientists will continue to study the Zharkov mammoth. They hope to discover how the mammoth died. This information may help them learn why mammoths became extinct.

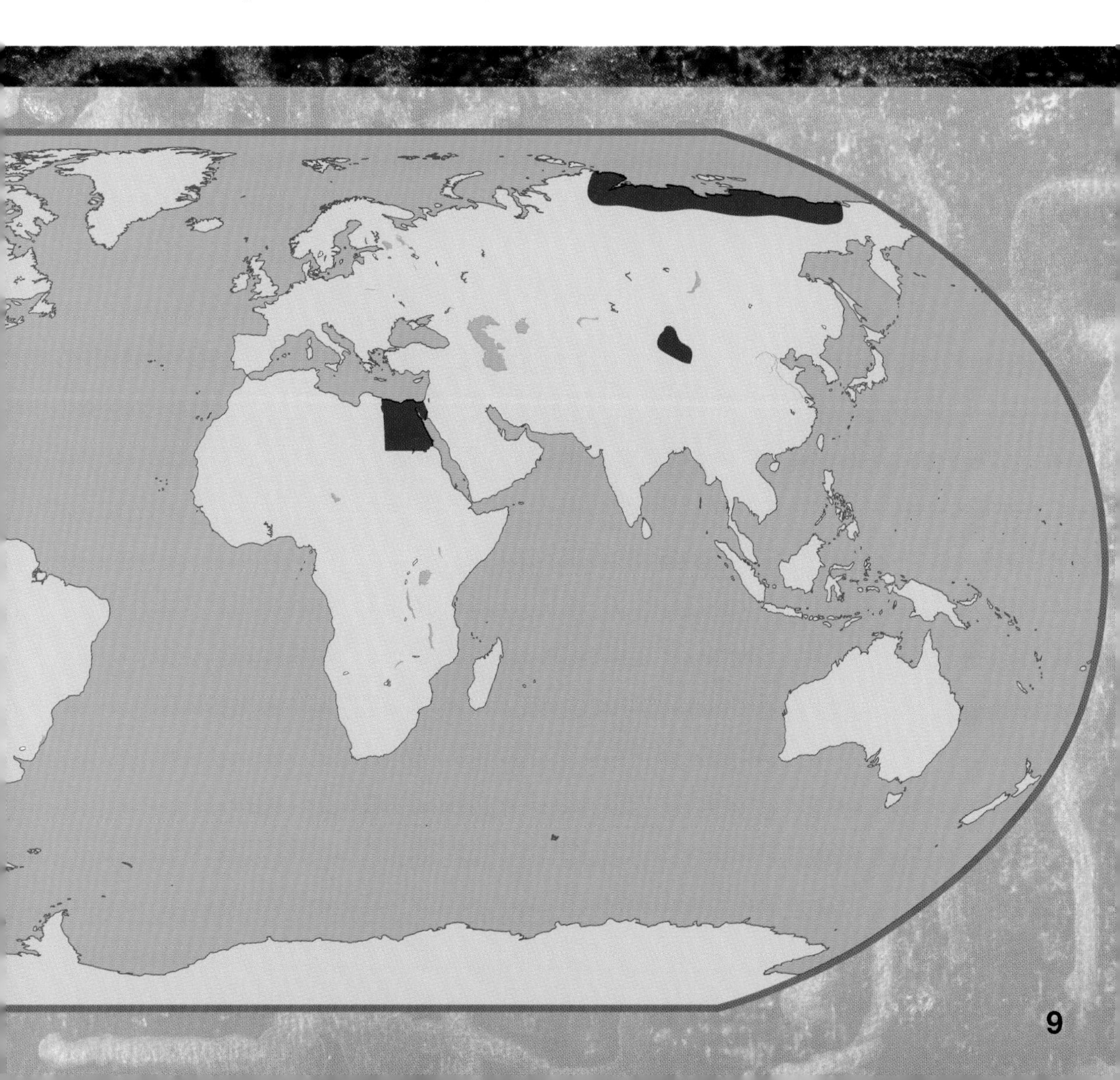

Learn About:

- Animal mummy features
- How animal mummies form
- Ancient beliefs about animals

A miner discovered this bison in Alaska. Scientists named it Blue Babe.

Chapter Two

How Animals Become Mummies

All living things decay after death. Small organisms called bacteria and fungi eat a dead body's tissues. The tissues then break down until only the bones remain.

A mummy forms when a body does not decay. Conditions can prevent bacteria and fungi from growing on bodies. These bodies sometimes become mummies. Mummies may have skin and eyes. They also may contain organs such as the heart and liver.

In 1977, a worker discovered Dima in Siberia.

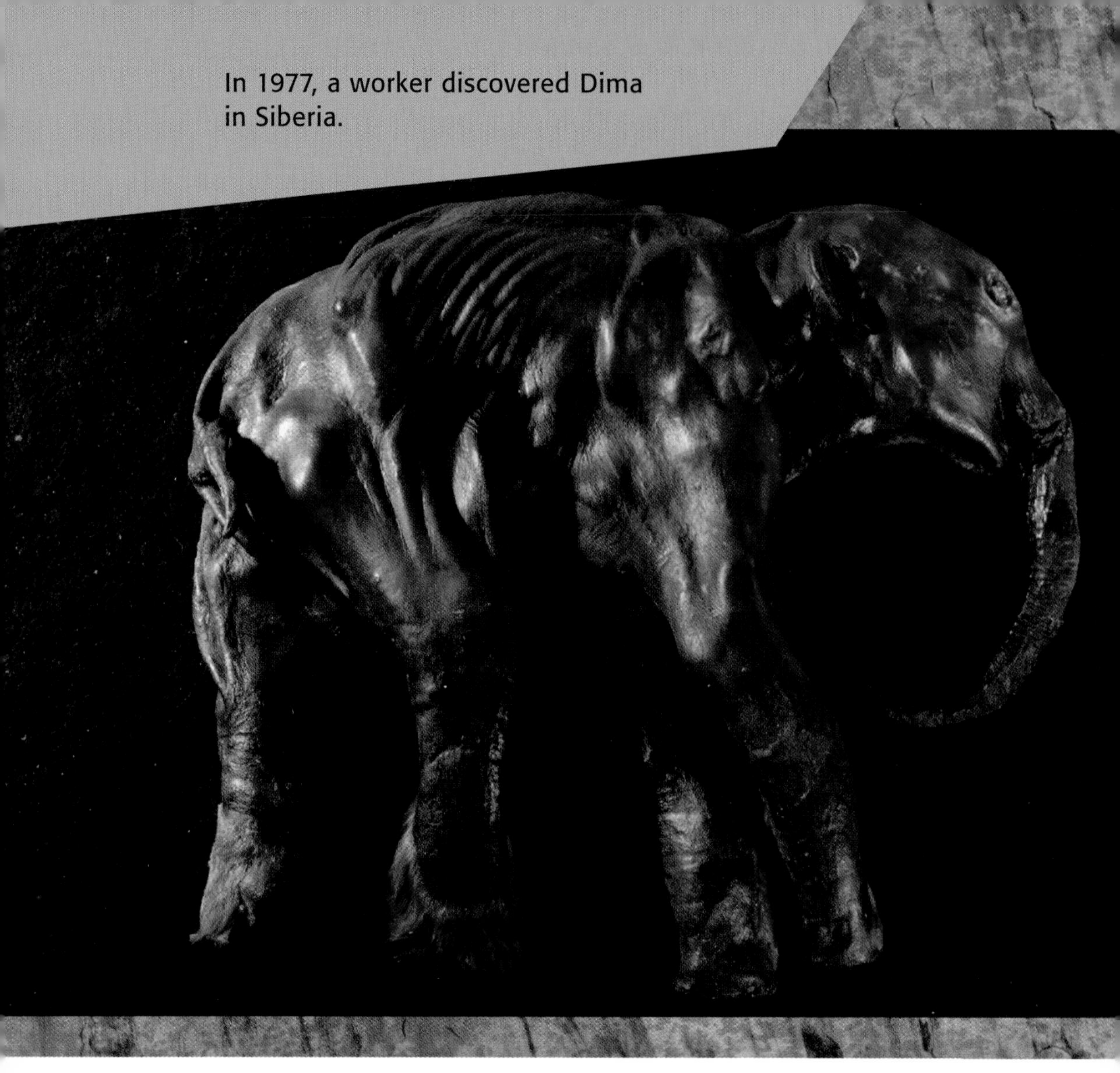

Frozen Animal Mummies

Natural conditions preserve many animal mummies. Bacteria and fungi cannot grow in freezing conditions. A body that freezes soon after death will not decay until its temperature rises above 32 degrees Fahrenheit (0 degrees Celsius).

Thousands of frozen animal mummies exist in the polar regions. These animals include mammoths, seals, squirrels, horses, and rhinoceroses. In 1977, a bulldozer operator found a young mammoth mummy in Siberia. Scientists named it Dima. In 1988, a ship captain found another young mammoth mummy near Siberia's northern coast.

In 1979, a miner discovered a frozen bison in Alaska. These large, hairy animals also are called buffalo. The mummy was a steppe bison. This type of bison is extinct. Scientists named the bison Blue Babe. Minerals in the soil had turned the bison's skin blue.

Mammoth Myths

Ancient Asians often found mammoth mummies or skeletons beneath the ice or frozen ground. Some of these ancient people believed mammoths were monsters that lived underground. They thought the huge creatures died when they came into sunlight. Other ancient people thought mammoths were giant moles that lived beneath the earth.

Ancient Mountain Burial

Cold mountain conditions have preserved horses in central Asia. Scientists believe some of these horses had belonged to people in an ancient tribe called the Pazyryk. These people lived in and near the Altai Mountains in southern Russia near its border with China. The Pazyryk lived in this area 2,200 to 2,700 years ago. They used horses to travel in the mountains.

Russian scientists discovered a Pazyryk woman's grave in 1993. They found six horse mummies wearing gold harnesses in the grave. It appeared the horses were hit in the head to kill them. Rain or melted snow flooded the grave soon after the woman and the horses were buried. The water then turned to ice and preserved the bodies.

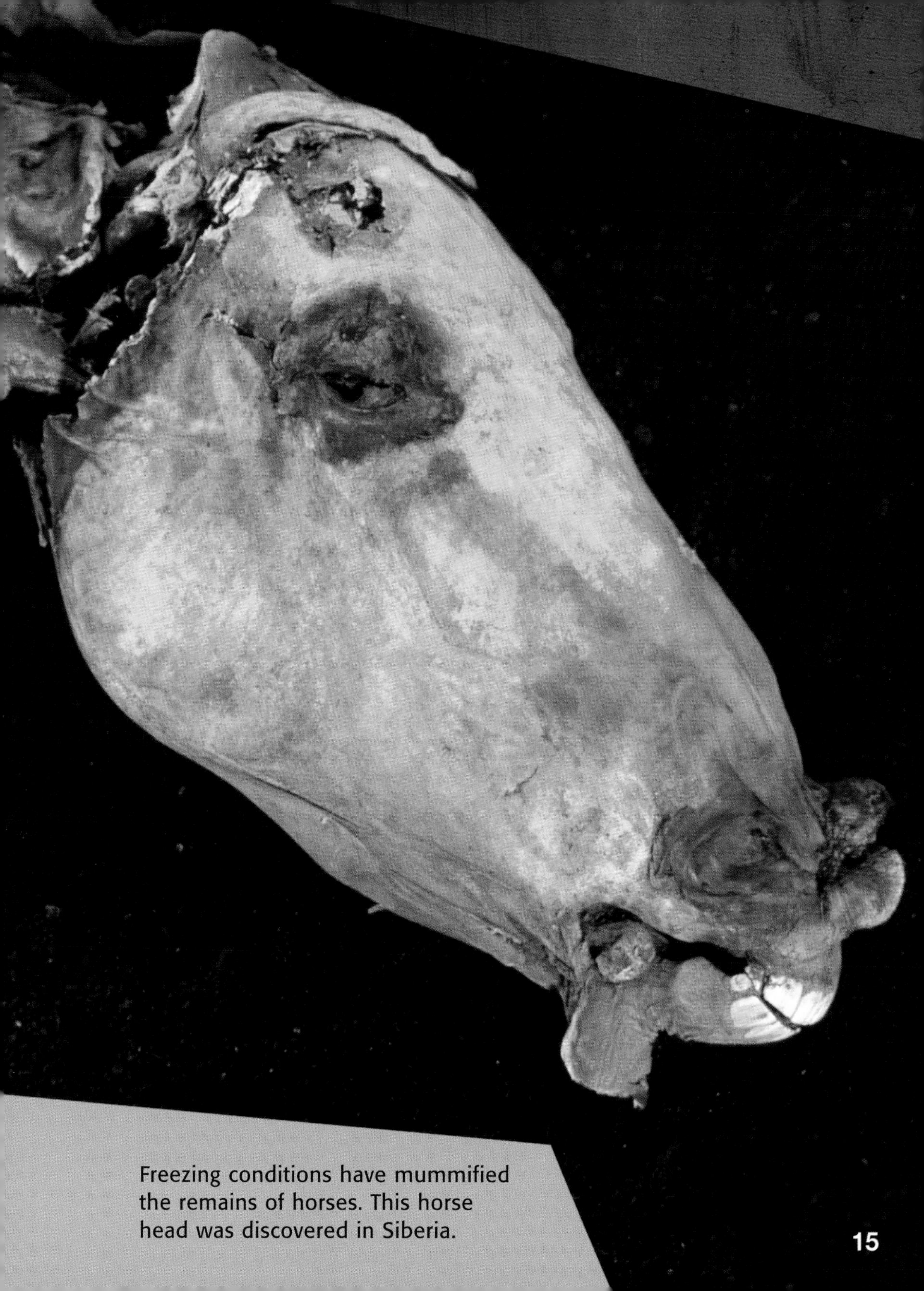

Freezing conditions have mummified the remains of horses. This horse head was discovered in Siberia.

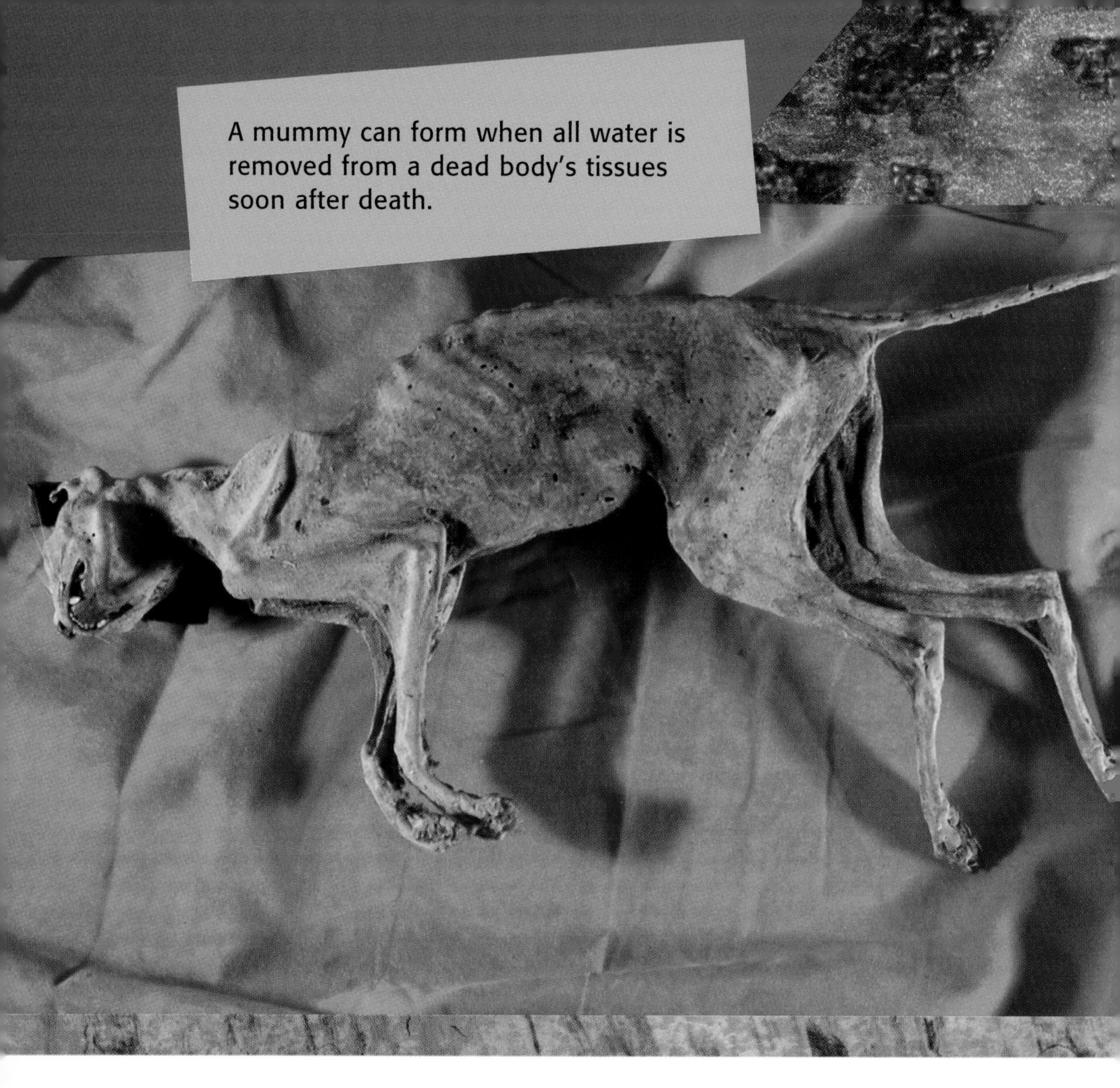

A mummy can form when all water is removed from a dead body's tissues soon after death.

Dried Animal Mummies

Hot, dry conditions also can cause animals to mummify. Without water, bacteria and fungi cannot grow in a dead body's tissues.

In 1907, people discovered two dog mummies in White Dog Cave. This cave is located in northeastern Arizona. The dogs were buried in a human grave. Dry conditions in the cave prevented the dogs' bodies from decaying. Scientists believe the two dogs died about 2,000 years ago.

Mummies Made by People

People have created many animal mummies. The ancient Egyptians mummified millions of animals. From about 3000 B.C. to A.D. 280, animal mummies were an important part of their religious beliefs.

The largest animal cemetery in Egypt is at Saqqara. Large tombs are located in this region of northern Egypt. Scientists guess more than one million animal mummies may be buried there.

The Paracas people of Peru also mummified animals. This group lived 2,000 to 3,000 years ago on the northwestern coast of South America. The Paracas placed the animals' bodies in baskets and buried them in underground tombs. Scientists have discovered dog, cat, parrot, deer, and frog mummies in these tombs.

Learn About:

- The ancient Egyptians
- The embalming process
- Kinds of ancient Egyptian animal mummies

The ancient Egyptians mummified millions of cats.

Chapter Three

Animal Mummies of Egypt

The ancient Egyptians mummified people and animals for more than 3,000 years. They mummified more animals than any other group of people on Earth.

Embalming Process

The ancient Egyptians used a process called embalming to make mummies. Embalmers followed several steps to preserve the bodies.

The embalmers first removed many of the animal's organs. These parts included the liver, stomach, and intestines. Embalmers then packed the body with a type of salt called natron. The natron soaked up water from the body's tissues.

Embalmers then poured warm resin over the body. This sticky substance comes from the sap of some trees. It prevented the body from becoming wet again.

The embalmers wrapped the animal with layers of cloth bandages and resin. After the resin dried and hardened, artists sometimes decorated the bandages.

Animals as Pets

The ancient Egyptians kept many animals as pets. Their pets included dogs, cats, monkeys, and small, horned animals called gazelles. Many ancient Egyptians believed they could be with their pets in another world after death. They thought they needed to preserve their pets' bodies for this reunion to happen.

Some ancient Egyptian pet owners had graves prepared for themselves and their pets. After a pet died, its owner had it made into a mummy. The owner then had the pet placed in the prepared grave.

Some owners died before their pets did. The ancient Egyptians placed the owners in their graves. Later, they sometimes made the pets into mummies and placed them with the owners.

The ancient Egyptians made many dogs into animal mummies.

Animals of Worship

The ancient Egyptians worshiped many gods. They believed a certain animal represented each god. For example, cats represented the goddess Bastet. Waterbirds called ibises represented the god Toth.

The ancient Egyptians took special care of these animals. They mummified the animals after they died. The ancient Egyptians made millions of cat, crocodile, bird, dog, and bull mummies to worship gods. They placed the mummies in underground tombs reserved for honored animals.

Empty Cases

Ancient Egyptian embalmers sometimes did not have enough animals. Scientists believe embalmers sometimes sold mummy cases containing no animals. The cases instead contained feathers, bones, bits of cloth, or pieces of clay. The buyers probably did not know they were buying fake mummies.

Gifts for the Gods

Ancient Egyptians also made animals into mummies as sacrifices. They offered these mummies to the gods as gifts. They thought the animals brought prayers to the gods.

Priests made sacrificial animal mummies in special temples. They often raised the animals intended for sacrifice and later killed them. Millions of dogs, cats, birds, and fish became mummy sacrifices to gods.

People bought animal mummies from the priests. They then brought the mummies to a cemetery located near a god's temple.

The ancient Egyptians often mummified crocodiles to honor the god Sobek.

Learn About:

- How people destroyed mummies
- Protecting existing animal mummies
- The Egyptian Museum

Today, people can view ancient Egyptian animal mummies in museums.

Chapter Four

Animal Mummies in Danger

By about A.D. 300, few Egyptians worshiped gods. The Romans had taken over Egypt. Most Egyptians had become Christians as the Romans had. These Egyptians no longer wanted to make mummies.

Throughout the next 1,000 years, various other groups ruled Egypt. Animal mummies were no longer valued. Some people robbed ancient Egyptian graves and cemeteries. The ancient Egyptians had often buried treasures with human and animal mummies.

Modern Mummies

Not all animal mummies are ancient. Today, some companies make people's pets into mummies. The companies use cloth and resin in a process similar to the one used by the ancient Egyptians. Some of these companies then put the mummy in a bronze case. These mummies are expensive. They may cost as much as $10,000 to $15,000.

Mummies Destroyed

In the Middle Ages (A.D. 476–1476), many Europeans destroyed both human and animal mummies. They used some of the human mummies to make medicine. This practice continued into the 1700s.

During the 1800s, Egyptians sold human and animal mummies to visitors. People conducted shows where they unwrapped human mummies. They charged others money to watch the shows.

In the late 1800s, people living in one Egyptian town shipped at least 28 tons (25 metric tons) of cat mummies to England. In England, people chopped up the mummies and sold them to farmers. The farmers spread the mummified remains on fields as fertilizer. They thought the mummy parts would help their crops grow.

Scientists keep most mummies in museums to protect them. This mummified dog is located in a museum in Pompeii, Italy.

Protecting Mummies

Today, most people respect mummies. They know mummies can help people learn about the past.

Scientists protect most mummies in museums. Mummies can decay after people remove them from their original locations. The Egyptian Museum in Cairo, Egypt, holds the largest collection of animal mummies in the world. A team of American, Pakistani, Egyptian, and British scientists is working to design a new room for these mummies. The animal mummies will be in special protective cases. The cases will protect the mummies from moisture, insects, and other damage. The scientists hope the new room will help preserve the ancient animal mummies for years to come.

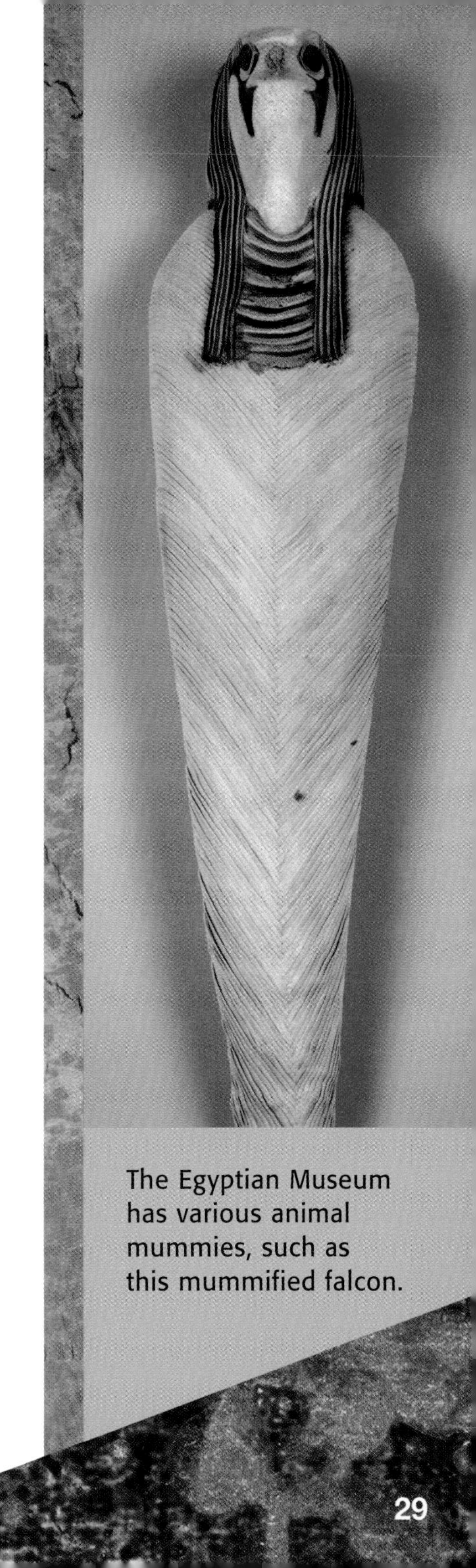

The Egyptian Museum has various animal mummies, such as this mummified falcon.

Words to Know

bacteria (bak-TIHR-ee-uh)—very small organisms; bacteria eat the soft tissue of dead bodies.

embalm (im-BAWLM)—to preserve a dead body so it does not decay

fungi (FUHN-jye)—a type of organism that has no leaves, flowers, or roots

gazelle (guh-ZEL)—a small antelope that lives in Asia and Africa

ibis (EYE-buhss)—a tall, slender bird that lives in and near ponds and lakes

natron (NAY-trawn)—a type of salt; the ancient Egyptians used natron to embalm bodies.

organism (OR-guh-niz-uhm)—a living plant or animal

resin (REZ-in)—a sticky substance that comes from the sap of some trees

To Learn More

Brier, Bob. *The Encyclopedia of Mummies.* New York: Facts on File, 1998.

Llewellyn, Claire. *The Big Book of Mummies: All about Preserved Bodies from Long Ago.* Lincolnwood, Ill.: Peter Bedrick Books, 2001.

Wilcox, Charlotte. *Mummies, Bones, and Body Parts.* Minneapolis: Carolrhoda Books, 2000.

Places of Interest

The Egyptian Museum
Tahrir Square
Cairo, Egypt

National Museum of Natural History
Smithsonian Institution
10th Street and Constitution Avenue NW
Washington, DC 20560

University of Pennsylvania Museum
33rd and Spruce Streets
Philadelphia, PA 19104

Internet Sites

The Animal Mummy Project in the Cairo Museum
http://www.animalmummies.com

DiscoverySchool.com—Woolly Mammoth
http://school.discovery.com/schooladventures/woolly
mammoth

Unwrapped: The Mysterious World of Mummies
http://tlc.discovery.com/tlcpages/mummies/
mummies.html

Index